The Earthen Skin

Ed Parris

Cover Art: *Adam and Eves*, Albrecht Durer, 1507.

Sabella Press

PO Box 95-51
Stanwood, WA 98292-0095

www.sabellapress.org

ISBN 0-9727039-2-6

The Earthen Skin

1   To the woodland choir
2   A child draws a circle
3   If I were sky
5   At a time
6   The ancient ones
7   I awoke
8   The first people
9   And then
10 The stone souls
11 When wooden houses
12 A man buried
13 The land
14 They came
17 Such beauty
18 Did anyone know the name
19 A child
20 A hand full of seed
21 Aim
22 As long as two fish
23 Did I call you into the room
24 Imagine pioneer women
25 Life's jazz
26 Like slicing eggplant
27 Like turning red in autumn
28 Listen to the rain
29 Little more that a gnat
30 Look at all this
31 Next time you swallow water
32 This low mist
33 The bones
34 What face he had
35 When I was four and we went to Yellowstone
36 Why must we let the sky

37   Green beads

38   Let us borrow

39   Mysterious of mind

40   The satin moonlight

41   The long autumn fingers

42   When two feet

43   She held pink hair ribbons

44   A line drawn on paper

45   The reason

46   Lavender scented sunrise in spring

47   When you return home

48   Candles on a cake

49   Who taught the wind

50   She walks

51   First light

52   On an aspen tree

53   Diving

54   A rock

55   On roads

56   An ankle-high cactus

57   A hummingbird

58   An autumn sunrise

59   Wild horses

60   Wind folds

61   The oldest doe

62   Above a mountain side

63   The elk

64   His howl calls out

65   They meet at the street-corner

66   It was one of those moons

67   When the sun goes down in the sea

68   Oh no, not in October

69   The river

The Earthen Skin

To the woodland choir,

the cricket chirp,
the deep frog ribet,

the owling
of hoo—

add the touch
of the earthen skin.

A child draws a circle

and draws into that universe
a tree and a dog and a cat,

And a bird in the tree
with a worm,

and full bloomed
a lover comes into her circle

unfolding the universe
from a child's eye.

If I were sky

and you sea,
my eyes would dance

on your skin
forever like starlight.

At a time

when this soil was nitrogen
rich from the bones
of fallen beasts

the ancient redwoods
gathered around me
and whispered

the entire history of earth
through their leaves,
and I took it all

into my sap
and through every vein
to the very tips

of my limbs.
Now I live for the wind
to sing from my leaves.

The ancient ones

heavy with snow
and winter wind
would lie themselves

down at our roots
for the food
of the species.

I grew my roots
into the rings
of their hearts.

I awoke

from my first dormant winter
to find sweet spring
caressing my bark, dancing

sweetly around and through
me until my budding leaves
opened and reached to her

and we sang each night,
the sweet wind and my green
leaves. With each new leaf,

the song grew fuller, each
new season, more precise,
more and more like love.

The first people

to walk this land
called bears their brothers
and begged forgiveness

for stealing their skins;
the bear-skinned people
grew cold and asked

the ancient ones for the gift
of fire and fire
they received.

I felt the heat
of the ancient ones
bleeding from me.

And then

the deer skinned people came
and their numbers
melted with the snow,

so, without asking,
they ravished our root-beds
and cut our flesh

into homes, leaving
the ancient spirit rings
to turn to stone.

The stone souls

were gathered
by cotton-clad people
who crushed them

and burned them
into glass, brick, steel.
They took the last

of the ancient ones
from my roots,
and although the wind

still sings through my leaves,
there are no saplings
to absorb the song

or grow their roots
into my heart,
there is no place

to lie down,
no young souls
to feed myself to.

When wooden houses

came no closer than the river,
young lovers at my roots
would lie their dreams

and promises and grow tense
in wool and satin—look close—
look deep into my bark

to see the ancient shape
of all that remains
of the young lovers' hearts.

A man buried

in a black beard brought his wife
and cut away my brothers to build
her a home in my shade.

She bore sons who tied a rope
to my limb to swing, but they grew
older and away. The man buried

her in my shade, burned my brothers,
and slumped toward the river,
a gray bearded shell. I grew

roots into her flesh
to find her love
and make it sing through my leaves.

The land

was abuzz with men
who had saws that buzzed
cleanly through trees,

precisely, heartlessly.
A man told his son,
"Look boy, each ring

is a year in the life
of a tree." In the next
season, Grandfather Redwood

fell across the same man,
and before his people
could find him, my roots

had grown into his intestines:
"Look boy, each fold is a year
in the life of a man."

They came

first on their feet,
then on horses, then
in wagons, in ships,

in trains, in cars,
in planes, and they
came to build their homes,

their churches, schools,
jails, stores, saloons,
K-Marts, Dairy Queens,

alcohol recovery centers,
and to build the New
York Stock Exchange.

Such beauty,

secluded bay with sand
towered by cedars,

more than one heart beats
the rhythm of waves.

A place like this can last forever
in light, should light be love.

The silhouette of young lovers
beamed light-years through space

shines back on the old and lonely
who once called this star

ourselves on a secluded bay
with sand towered by cedars.

Did anyone know the name

you took from the wind
that rippled the bay?

Did anyone who saw you in the light
see the light in you?

Did anyone understand a fire so hot
it could only be captured in ice?

A child

in new shoes went
with his mother and a new guy

to a new place with a new net to catch
a new butterfly for his jar,

which he dropped and broke
on the way home

and the new guy laughed
as the butterfly flew away.

Years later, his mother
did not remember that new guy's name,

nor where that place was
but her ashes would like to be

with that butterfly. A lonely man
remembered Converse All-Stars

while searching for lost things,
lost places, lost moments,

lost people
clutching a new urn.

A hand full of seed

is all it takes
to make the birds dance

on a gray mid-February
Sunday; one hand

clenching seed, the other
open to possibilities

of attendant angels
flying wreaths around

their beloved queen.

Aim

your headlights true—
true to dream, true to love,

true to life and beyond—
for that created in light

shall never cease, shall be
the aurora of your soul.

As long as two fish

swim in the sea,
clouds gather on the horizon

where the glories of geese
are sung to the rising moon,

the sun crosses the island
each day; as long

as yonder trees grow —
that's how long.

Did I call you into the room?

This? A room of endless night,
a crescent of gold portraying moon,

twink of silvering stars,
angel feather floating cloud.

Let me awaken you to this
glow upon clean pink skin

where all the world's poetry,
the song of man, the dance of woman

come down to a single molecule
where the golden moonlight shines

on you, on me,
and all life,

the silvering gold
feather of life.

Imagine pioneer women

singing cradle songs
in lumbering Calistoga.

Imagine them in the heat,
flies and dust, iron wagon wheels

tumble-bumping
rut-to-rut.

Imagine the hold
they have on their babies.

Imagine them in long beard,
burly men with bear-paw hands

who yet are soft, sweet babies
safe in the mother arms

of this tumble-bumping
rut-to-rut world. Imagine

the ox-drawn Calistoga
reins in your hands. Yours

is the cargo of flesh, of soul,
of dream, and of tumble-bumping hope.

Life's jazz

glistens upon a wave,
a fluttering heart valve

illuminated in ultrasound,
a familiar hand waves

in the rear window
of Heaven's bus: *Goodbye.*

Like slicing eggplant

you could explore the brain
of a plumber who understands

the work of a pump
and would know the heart well,

but the soul,
neither preserved in a jar

or captured in ice,
can not be known completely.

There are no folded convolutions,
chambers or valves,

no fleshy growths
or imperfections with age,

no birth, no death—
it is no more real

than the honey scent of gardenia
the push and pull of tides;

the undying soul is no more to a man
than flight to a bird.

Like turning red in autumn,

we must all endure, be braced
for winter, welcome the cold

into our veins like the leaf
welcomes the fall.

Listen to the rain

with your eyes closed, mind open,
heartbeat sympathetic. Listen

for the splash tones of speech,
absent of consonant or vowel

or any namable thing
as if listening from the womb.

Listen to that voice
from deep within yourself

that speaks this perfect language—
sympathetic splash tones of rain.

Little more than a gnat,

something less of a fly
paused and buzzed

like a word
on the tip of a brain

waiting to be said,
then flew.

Look at all this

stuff God has to do—
you can't bother him

with your bald tires,
your unsightly cellulite,

your need for a new car,
reliable cellular service,

low interest financing
and glasses. God

has better things to do.
Take your ass to Costco.

Next time you swallow water,

feel water in your mouth. A spring
trickles from rock, cuts a frozen path

in the snow. In your throat
and beyond, life's river

and all its tributaries
lead to the love lake of your soul.

Ahh. Taste water.

This low mist

at the shoreline
erases the sea

as if the earth just
ends, that's it. Over.

There is nothing
beyond the mist

except the distant
moaning of gulls.

The bones

of bare tree shiver
in the ice-blue wind

whistling
from sea to mountain

across white meadow
to this place

where bundled children
make angels.

What face he had

shining through gray beard
was beaten red by weather and light,

eyes white-washed by rain,
and he held a small sign:

Viet Nam vet —
will work for beer.

When I was four and we went to Yellowstone

the trees were tall and the cars
bumper to bumper, and it was hot—

Chicago with trees—and a big
one-eared bear reached in

the passenger-side window
and took the Oreos right off my lap.

Why must we let the sky

hold us down so?
Why not sprout Victorian wings,

fly among planets and stars
and such things other world

and pity sure-footed folk
of such limited flight—huh?

Why not?

Green beads

at the blue horizon
purpled by sunburst

sunset. Beads,
green, blue, purple

drape the brown
bosom of earth.

Let us borrow

from this tree the leaf,
auburn curls of hair against

the pearl backdrop sky—
soft, round shoulders,

smooth white flesh;
borrow from this sea

the ebb and flow of a blue
gown that falls at sunset

to the earthen floor,
the moon tides.

Mysterious of mind,

glorious of body, she escapes
on the soft wings of morning

into those hot arms:
all that is left is sun.

The satin moonlight

on rippled water.
Two bodies, one heartbeat:

the reason they live.

The long autumn fingers

of the quaking ash reach
to the color blending sky—

this is the blue, grey,
purple, pink whiteness

of lover's hands
on the glass at an airport

watching the other
in a silver streak

be lifted away.

When two feet,

two hands, two ears,
two eyes, one torso,

one head, one determined heart
and one infinite mind

find glory in another
two feet, two hands,

two ears, two eyes,
one torso, one head,

another accepting heart,
another giving mind—

a single body explodes
from the molten core

of the love tumbling earth.

She held pink hair ribbons

against the summer sky
and saw rainbows of her own design,

and she was just eight.
Eighteen and packing

for Sarah Lawrence,
those same ribbons

beneath the bathroom sink,
a little frayed, some mold,

an umbilical thing
left behind, she goes away.

A line drawn on paper,

the first connecting dot
to a star and another star

and another star,
until the archer

with eternal aim, draws
upon a silver brush

in golden hair, satin draped
shoulders in an antique mirror.

The reason

birds whistle in spring,
tides follow the moon

on star speckled summer nights,
owls ask who in autumn frost,

snowflakes dance like swans,
a person finds peace

upon a lover's breast.

Lavender scented sunrise in spring,

mid-May to be exact—
exactly in the middle

of a man's mid-May life,
morning, like a lover from her bath,

has risen.

When you return home

after many years
it is as if

Elm Street never changed.
The yard still has the picket fence,

white paint chipped,
the gate a little lame.

The Radio Flyer in the front yard
is still missing one wheel.

There are cobwebs inside,
but down to the blue checked drapes

it is as if
Elm Street never changed.

On the table a mixing bowl
with two wooden spoons,

you use one as a wand
and cast a little spell.

You never thought coming home
would be so real. *Cut!*

*That's a wrap! Be back on set
Monday morning—6AM.*

Candles on a cake,

several empty bottles
of chardonnay,

a platter
to collect the bones.

Who taught the wind

to push his weight around?
Why don't the trees push back?

The trees, the sea, the clouds,
the mountains, the sun—

why don't they all just push back?

She walks

and learned to walk on stone walks
sunken into soft earth by a history of men
whose grandest plans were to walk on stone,

but on those walks she found only sunken
foundations for iron factories, prisons, tv
stations: stone slabs of ambitious dreams

that she steps out of naked beneath
a blue raincoat, barefeet buried in mud,
tears sunken into and mistaken for skin.

First light

spreads like morning blood
across the lake while birds

sing out from a leafy stage

and a fish blows kisses
to the vanishing moon.

He said

the dog liked to call his name
to all who passed,

and the dog's name was Ralph.
Ralph! Ralph! He said

the dog knew his name
connected him to earth,

made him distinct,
recognizable as say,

the sea. He tied sea kelp
around the dog's neck

so that the sea
would remember the dog

when it heard his name:
Ralph! Ralph!

Diving

dolphins stitch in
and out of the waves,

sewing
broken pieces of sea.

A rock

about the size of a brain
is a sharp contrast

to the white-gold beach
where a lapping wave
falls flat, licks the sand
around this cool lava

broken free from the flow.
Oh, how the island grows!

On roads

where there are no cars,
in deserts

where there are no homes,
up on poles,

wires buzz.

An ankle-high cactus

holds a blue rose
to the east and a red

rose to the west
and sleeps all day

in the purple shade.

A hummingbird

flutters before a white rose
and lives forever

in the purple sunrise.

An autumn sunrise

rises above the mountains
that rise up beyond the lake's

horizon, and reflects in the eyes
of an old bear who just yawns.

Wild horses

stop their wild work
and turn tails to the wind

while clouds billow
purple layer upon black

at the horizon of a storm
and darkness bleeds into daylight.

Lightning strikes the sky blue
and wind begins to blow;

rain drives the wild horses
to stand close and slow.

Wind folds

layer upon layer of icy snow
upon snow

across the frozen face
of the mountain that waits

for spring to weep, each tear
a finger of stream that joins

the river's arm and buries
winter in the hot, salty heart.

The oldest doe,

her nose to the wind,
remembers gun powder,

Marlboro and Budweiser,
and what this cold air means.

Above a mountain side

dotted with stumps, a hawk
circles and searches

but finds only dust.
Not earth nourished

by fallen leaves,
nor flowering bush

pollinated by bees;
No shade, no stable root,

no towering pine, no
home, no home.

No home.

The elk

above the timberline
sees the distant lights,

the peopled world creeping closer,
and he shudders to know

that he wears the family tree
of *Cervis Canadensis*

upon his own head.

His howl calls out

to all who live beneath this moon:
I am coyote

and I walk alone tonight.
Only his echo returns:

I walk alone tonight
and I am coyote.

They meet at the street-corner

newsstand, buying the morning paper,
and chat while small angels escape

their breath, hover above them.
One is going aluminum this year

but will wait until after Christmas
when prices are down, so this

will be the last year of real trees.
The other has long since given up

on trees and would like to escape
this winter ritual, but when they part,

opposite directions, each has an angel
hovering above each breath.

It was one of those moons—

a thumbnail thing
piercing cloud,

illuminating
ring.

Illuminating
thing piercing

a cloud with the light
of one of those thumbnail moons.

When the sun goes down in the sea

where does it go? Does it call
on the whales for afternoon tea?

Perhaps bologna sandwiches and tea,
maybe some of those lobster fingers

and a glass of merlot. They have a good time—
the sun and the whales in the sea.

Oh no, not in October,

not when trickster fog
blends sky, sea, earth

into an autumn tea,
not now shall we deal

with the intrusions of Mr. Death,
not now. Oh let this cold

tea of autumn mist condensed
on the window at morning break

be the bare dew of life,
passion on a lover's brow,

sunrise where the sun meets
the sea the color of a kiss,

snow caps, bare trees,
fingers tremble at the breast.

The river

speaks to the stars and moon:
I shall carry your light

on my rippled surface forever —
we shall never be alone.

Ed Parris

Ed Parris was born in Chicago is 1956, but has spent most of his life in the Pacific Northwest. He holds an AA degree from Windward Community College, a BA from the University of Hawaii at Manoa, and an MFA from Eastern Washington University. His work has appeared in *The New York Quarterly, Blueline, Colorado Review, Hawaii Review, Mangraove, Rain Bird, Slipstream, Poets On, Poetry Motel, Black Warrior Review,* and others. A previous book, *The Boy in the Bushes,* was published by Mellon Poetry Press in 1996.